Silke Alles   Sieglinde Janzen

Healthy Breads
with the
Breadmaker

Delicious and nutritious bread creations

alive books

Vancouver
Canada

Contents

All About Bread

Healthy Recipes

Note: Conversions in this book (from imperial to metric) are not exact. They have been rounded to the nearest measurement for convenience. Exact measurements are given in imperial. The recipes in this book are by no means to be taken as therapeutic. They simply promote the philosophy of both the author and *alive* books in relation to whole foods, health and nutrition, while incorporating the practical advice given by the author in the first section of the book.

All About Bread

Breadmaking is an art and the baker has the power to make it a healthful masterpiece.

So you think your life was difficult before the invention of the breadmaker? The Egyptians used their feet to knead bread dough and their hands to mix mortar!

Introduction . . . .

There is nothing more wonderful than waking up to the aroma of freshly baked bread!

Traditionally, this was only possible if mother got up at four in the morning to begin the long process.

Today, with a breadmaker, it's possible to have both freshly baked bread and a good night's sleep. The invention of the breadmaker allows us, through saved time and labor, to experiment with our bread creations. The variations are seemingly endless, unlike the variety offered at the supermarket, or even the bakery. With all of the different fruits, nuts, vegetables, herbs, grains and oils available to us, there is no reason to make or eat plain bread.

Experimenting with ingredients and methods of bread baking can result in wonderfully nutritious and delicious surprises for your family and friends: fruity bread with cherries today, a nutty bread with pecans tomorrow and a classic bread for the toaster the next day. Whichever you choose, your day can begin with warm, healthy bread.

Healthful, nutritious bread begins with wisely chosen ingredients—whole grain flours, healthy oils and nutritious additions. The knowledge, advice, tips and recipes that follow will encourage and motivate you to create in the tastiest and healthiest way possible.

White Bread is Dead ...

Refined white flour has been denatured and bleached and, as a result, contains about as much nutritional value as cardboard. The body must metabolize this empty food and can only do so by using stored vitamins and minerals. Eating bread made with demineralized white flour robs the body of calcium. Poor bone health and deterioration of teeth are the results. Constipation, colon cancer, diabetes and many other chronic ailments are linked to eating white, denatured, fiberless breads and other products.

Whole grains lose a significant amount of their nutrients during the refining process.

Refining takes place in order to prolong the shelf-life of the flour, and the bread from which it's made. The grain is "cleansed" of all perishable components that will deteriorate and hinder machine processing. The vitamin- and mineral-rich parts of the kernel, the oil-rich germ and the valuable bran are separated during this process and are used for cattle feed! Whole grain loses 10 to 100 percent of its vitamin, mineral and fiber content during the commercial milling and refining process.

All flour is made from grain, however, they are not all whole grain flours! All-purpose white flour is stripped of much of its composition. The end product is an excellent source of gluten (that's why it still works in bread baking) but it definitely no longer consists of whole grains.

Since the human body cannot live by protein and starch alone, the flour is then "enriched" with chemical vitamins and minerals, which are not easily absorbed by the body. Niacin, riboflavin, thiamin and iron are added back into refined white flour, but all the other nutrients remain lost forever.

The end result is that the grain has been stripped of its nutrients, given a few back and labeled "enriched" so consumers think they're buying a quality product. People are so used to buying white flour and eating white bread that they

actually believe it is wholesome and natural, however, that couldn't be farther from the truth.

White, refined flour has a higher ratio of gluten, which has shown to inhibit peristalsis of the intestinal tract, resulting in chronic constipation when eaten regularly. The general public may not consider themselves constipated unless they go days without a bowel movement. In reality, those who eat a whole foods diet, with plenty of fiber and true nutrients, have a bowel movement after each meal.

Because white flour lacks fiber, eating it can cause or contribute to constipation, diabetes, obesity, arteriosclerosis, gallbladder problems, skin disease and colon cancer. Fiber is necessary because it transports the bad cholesterol out of the body. The B-vitamin group, which is responsible for a well-functioning metabolism among many things, is lost during the refining process. If we look at the nutrients lost during the processing of flour, we can see the exact nutrients that are lacking in our daily nutrition.

People are so used to buying white flour and eating white bread that they actually believe it is wholesome and natural, however, that couldn't be farther from the truth.

Whole Grain Products are Healthier . . . . . .

Whole grains offer a variety of nutrients. All grains are high in carbohydrates that are easily converted into energy. Products prepared with whole grains have a superior nutritional value containing high amounts of protein, fiber (roughage), vitamins and minerals. Since these precious nutrients are concentrated in the outer membrane and the germ of the grain, it is important to eat the whole grain for better nutrition. Whole grains are not fattening, just more filling because of their nutritional value and fiber content.

Whole grains contain a high amount of insoluble fiber, which keeps the intestinal flora healthy and increases stool volume considerably. This is very important for health, because the increased volume of the stool speeds up the elimination process, decreasing the time it takes to travel through the intestinal tract. This, in turn, decreases the risk for chronic intestinal diseases, including cancer.

Bread prepared with natural organic whole grain flour might be more costly, but in the long run it saves medical costs on degenerative diseases such as arthritis, cancer, diabetes, heart problems, and many others.

Favorite Bread-Baking Grains

Amaranth is a vegetable, from which the seeds are exported as a grain. These seeds, which are rich in vitamins and minerals, are gaining popularity in North America.

Barley is traditionally used in Asia for bread baking, however, as it gains a reputation for being low in fat it is finding its way into North American bread as well.

Buckwheat (also known as kasha) is often used in breakfast foods such as pancakes and cereals, however, it isn't a true cereal grain. This high-protein and high-fiber grain is a perfectly good candidate for bread. It tastes wonderful and mixes well with wheat flour and other grains to increase the overall gluten content of the bread.

Corn is best when stone ground into flour from the whole kernel. As with cornmeal, which can also be used in bread recipes, it is usually a yellow color. Corn contains cancer-fighting agents as well as valuable vitamins and minerals.

Kamut is a grain that is usually well tolerated by wheat-sensitive people, although its gluten content is low, so it is often combined with a wheat flour.

Millet is used extensively throughout India. When added to bread it will deliver a crunch, added moisture and a subtle toasted flavor. Millet flour is a wonderful source of protein and is rich in minerals (especially iron, calcium, silica and zinc). The results are an energy-boosting bread.

Oats help to lower cholesterol, are high in protein and are a good

In North America, most barley is brewed for beer, most corn is fed to cattle and most millet is used as birdseed.

9

source of vitamin E. An oat flour will add a sweet flavor to your wheat breads.

Rice is even greater than wheat in global production. Nutritious rice flour made from long-grain and short-grain rice may be used in bread.

Rye is high in the essential amino acid lysine and is often used for flat breads and dense sandwich breads. However, when combined with a wheat flour, rye flour will make a bold-tasting, homemade-style loaf with a chewy crust. Because rye creates a heavier bread, add caraway seeds to help digestion, prevent bloating and add a wonderful taste and aroma.

Spelt is an ancient variety of wheat originating from Mesopotamia and Persia, which was used by the ancient Greeks and Romans. The baking properties of spelt do not differ much from those of wheat and can therefore be used in place of it for variety or by those with a wheat allergy. It is one of the easiest grains to digest and is high in B vitamins.

Facts on Flour . . . .

Flour is simply the powdery result of ground grains (and sometimes seeds). It, along with water and yeast, forms the basis of one of our basic food staples: bread.

Both hard winter wheat and hard spring wheat are considered good for bread baking, although the hard spring wheat, planted in the spring season in northern climates, has the most gluten, which is beneficial for a successful bread. Soft wheat has less gluten and is best used for recipes that don't rely on the gluten development factor, such as cakes and pastries.

Wheat and spelt flours contain the gluten necessary to make the bread rise. Other grain flours, however, do not rise on their own. Therefore to make leavened bread, you should always use about 20 percent wheat flour (unless, of course, you are gluten-intolerant).

Gluten

Not all grains are equal when it comes to gluten. It is the gluten, when mixed with liquid and then warmed, that works with the yeast to raise the bread. Without gluten, bread is flat and dense. Gluten is most evident in wheat, which explains why this versatile grain is popular.

Many stores now sell 5-grain and 7-grain mixes, or you can purchase a variety of basic grains and create your own mixtures. While ready-mixed baking flour is available at most health food stores, unless the flour is freshly milled it will always taste slightly bitter. This is because the oils from the wheat germ and cracked sunflower or flax seeds start to go rancid anywhere from a couple of days to three weeks after milling. For this reason alone it pays to have a flour mill in your kitchen. Freshly milled grains and ground oil seeds will give your bread an incomparable flavor and high nutritional value.

Why Organic Flour?

Bread is one of our most important staple foods. Since it is so often a part of our menu, we need to be aware of its contents.

It is very important to use organically grown grains whenever possible. The increased use of commercial chemical fertilizers causes hazardous substances to develop in the ground and the plant itself. The natural cell structure of the plant is altered. The cells that have absorbed the chemical fertilizer are less resistant to pests, which in turn leads to the application of toxic chemical pesticides. These pesticides not only kill the enemies of the plant, but harm the people that eat the harvested product.

Leaveners . . . .

The leavener is the ingredient in the bread that causes it to rise. This happens due to its reaction to both liquid and heat. The most common leaveners are baking powder and baking soda, eggs, fats and yeast. The leavener preferred by the majority of bread makers is yeast, probably one of the oldest leaveners used by humans. A single-celled living micro-organism, the yeast you buy must be "alive" to work—check the date on the package.

Children enjoy helping in the kitchen, which gives them a better understanding of nutrition.

Proper Proportions

If the bread doesn't turn out right it is usually because of improper proportions between the flour and the liquid.

When baking your own bread you have the creative power to make it exactly what you want it to be! You may add fresh or dried fruits, nuts, seeds and many other special and tasty touches to make your bread unique and healthful. Do not add more than 2 ½ ounces (70 grams) of fruit, nuts or seeds per loaf so you don't overwork the machine's motor. Some hard seeds and grains should be soaked overnight for easier processing in the machine.

Fruit

Finely chopped cherries, plums, apples, bananas and organic unsulfured dried fruit such as figs, apricots, dates, currants or raisins make wonderful and successful bread additions. Fruits, whether fresh or dried, are an important source of vitamins, minerals and roughage. Dark, unsulfured raisins are rich in potassium, phosphorus, magnesium, iron and calcium, and are a good source of A and B complex vitamins.

Cherries have blood-cleansing properties and work to improve the symptoms associated with gout and arthritis. Sweet cherries are a good source of vitamin C and tart cherries are a good source of vitamin A.

Organic, ripe bananas are richer in minerals than most other soft fruits, are an excellent source of potassium and are soothing to the intestines. Dried apricots are a good source of iron, and apples are an excellent source of pectin and fiber. Apple cider and fruit juices are also excellent additions.

The list of delicious fruits and their healthful properties is seemingly endless. Therefore, so are the opportunities for experimenting with them in bread recipes.

Vegetables

Don't forget your vegetables! This amazing nutritious family of food is full of vitamins, minerals and fiber. Vegetables or their

Fruit and vegetables are true vitamin and mineral bombs. No other food group has so many nutritional benefits.

12

pulp, paste or juice make wonderful additions to bread. Grated sundried tomatoes, carrots, sweet peppers, peeled and seeded cucumbers, zucchini, chives and onions are popular and fun additions. Carrot juice and tomato paste are also wonderful in bread.

Nuts and Seeds

Nuts and seeds are nutritional powerhouses. Nature provided them with all the nutrients necessary to grow large plants and trees. These same nutrients are very beneficial for humans as well. Nuts and seeds are rich in important nutrients such as protein, healthy fats, fiber, minerals and vitamins such as E, A, B_1 and B_2.

Ground flax seeds top them all in nutritional value. They contain mucilage, fiber, phyto-nutrients, essential fatty acids and constitute an almost perfect protein.

Sunflower seeds are nutritionally remarkable, containing proportionally more protein than beef, as well as essential fatty acids, calcium, phosphorus, iron and vitamins A, B, D and E.

The sesame seed has long been appreciated for its taste and nutritional benefits, especially in Mediterranean and Eastern civilizations. It contains more protein than any nut, as much iron as liver and is high in vitamin E. A few sesame seeds sprinkled on top of the crust of a bread not only adds nutrition and flavor but eye appeal as well.

Almost all nuts are suitable for bread baking. Walnuts, pecans, almonds, pistachios, pine nuts, macadamia nuts and cashews are favorites for their nutritional value and unbeatable taste.

Oils

While most breads can be baked without oil, bakers use it to help their dough rise. Oil also enhances the flavor of bread and helps to preserve it. If you like fluffy bread, oil will be your favorite addition to a recipe. The type of oil you add, however, is crucial.

Grinding flax seeds is easy and convenient with an electric coffee bean grinder.

Most cooking oils displayed in the supermarket are refined and should be absolutely avoided for bread baking and any other type of baking, cooking or even salad dressing. Margarine and shortening have no place in the healthy whole foods kitchen. Processed oils and hydrogenated (hardened) oils such as margarine and shortening are full of damaged fats, known as trans-fatty acids. They have been shown to be extremely detrimental to health and have even been linked to cancer. Many recipes nowadays recommend canola oil, the newest oil on the market. It is marketed as a heart healthy oil because the seeds have been genetically engineered to exclude erucic acid (a specific fatty acid associated with fibrotic heart lesions). However, there are indications that canola oil presents health problems on its own. During the high heat refining and deodorizing process, the healthy omega-3 fatty acids are changed into dangerous and unhealthy trans-fatty acids. Recent studies also show that canola oil has a high sulfur content and that regular consumption leads to vitamin E deficiency. And, believe it or not, traces of the erucic acid that causes heart lesions are still found in canola oil. Only unrefined, natural oils and natural butter should be used.

Personal communications, Mary G Enig, PhD

Sauer, F D, et al *Nutr Res*, 1997, 17:2:259-269

Kramer, J K G, et al, *Lipids*, 1982, 17:372-382; Trenholm, H L, *et al Can Inst Food Sci Technol J*, 1979, 12:189-193

Natural, unrefined coconut oil is a healthful bread baking ingredient.

Healthy, unprocessed seed oils provide the essential fatty acids our bodies need and can efficiently use. However, most of these are not heat stable and should not be used in baking. The oils most suitable for baking include coconut oil, almond oil, extra-virgin olive oil and sesame oil.

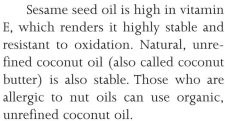

Sesame seed oil is high in vitamin E, which renders it highly stable and resistant to oxidation. Natural, unrefined coconut oil (also called coconut butter) is also stable. Those who are allergic to nut oils can use organic, unrefined coconut oil.

Do not use flax, pumpkin and walnut oil, as these will be damaged with heat. Whole flax seeds, however, are okay to use in bread baking. For complete and easy-to-understand information on this topic read *Good Fats and Oils* by Siegfried Gursche (*alive* Natural Health Guides, 2000).

Sea Salt

Salt adds yet more taste to your bread and helps to strengthen the crust. Choose a high-quality sea salt and use it sparingly. Sea salt does not affect the kidneys as common table salt does. Avoid iodized table salt because it has all the minerals washed and leached out of it. The sodium ions of table salt bind to water in cells, increasing pressure in the tissues and putting a strain on the heart, which can lead to high blood pressure. If iodine is needed, kelp is a much better source.

Herbs and Spices . . . .

All you need for new and wonderfully tasty bread each day is an imagination and the knowledge to choose healthful ingredients. Bread doesn't have to taste the same every day. Herbs and spices are a fantastic addition to bread and will guarantee a unique experience for your taste buds each time. Your stomach will be happy too, because herbs and spices also promote good digestion and help relieve bloating.

Fennel seed, with its mild taste and aroma, is one of the oldest bread baking spices.

15

Tasty and Beneficial

Caraway: Aids digestion of heavy, fatty foods and helps relieve bloating and stomach cramps. These seeds are mainly used for rye breads, which are more difficult to digest than wheat breads.

Fennel: Relieves stomach cramps and stimulates intestinal peristalsis.

Cinnamon: This spice adds a sweet touch to bread and is also a very nice addition to buns.

Cumin: Adds an Arabic flair to your bread. Use about ¼ teaspoon per loaf.

Star Anise: Excellent digestive aid and relieves bloating.

Thyme: Eliminates gas and reduces fever and headache.

We recommend buying spices and herbs whole when possible, not in powder or cut form, because crushed seeds and leaves, which contain the aroma and taste, quickly lose their essential oils. Buy spices in small quantities, to preserve their aromatic qualities and grind them yourself in an electric coffee mill just before adding them to the dough. Buy herbs fresh and cut them just before adding them to your recipe.

Spices not only enhance the aroma of bread but their essential oil content helps to preserve the bread, so it will last longer. Keep in mind, when using spices or herbs, that more does not necessarily mean better. In fact, if you can taste a specific spice you have used too much of it. No more than 1 or 2 teaspoons is needed. Mixing many different spices and herbs for one bread loaf is not advisable. One addition per loaf will bring out the spice's full potential and aroma.

Cheese and Kefir . . . .

Kefir is a popular fermented milk product in many parts of the world, and is now gaining status in the West as a delicious alternative to yogurt. Many of the recipes in *Liver Cleansing Handbook* (*alive* Natural Health Guides, 2000) call for kefir.

Adding cheese to bread recipes will give you surprisingly flavorful results. Use any of your favorite natural cheeses, grated or cut into small pieces. The best cheeses to mix into your dough are Swiss, Gruyère, Parmesan, Gouda and Cheddar.

Kefir not only lightens the dough, but adds nutritional value and enhances the taste.

- All ingredients should be added at room temperature.

- Whole wheat flour contains the germ of the wheat kernel, which is high in good, healthy fat. Whole wheat flour should be stored in a cool place (below 60°F/15°C) and used within one month, or frozen for longer storage to prevent them from going rancid. According to research done by Dr. Kollath, a German nutritional scientist, the milled flour has not only lost most of its nutritional value after six weeks of storage, but turns rancid when stored for a longer period of time, and may actually develop toxic substances through oxidation. It is best is to grind your own flour as needed. Buying a quality flour mill is certainly a good investment. It is also more economical to purchase grains in larger quantities and mill them when the flour is needed.

- Baked bread should be stored in a cool, dry and ventilated place to avoid the formation of mold. Only on very hot days will it require refrigeration. By the way, homemade bread does not mold as quickly as store-bought bread. In fact, according to some experts, store-bought bread is already moldy on the shelf because it is wrapped in plastic. The toxic mold on bread is usually not visible with the naked eye, and cannot be detected by taste. This mold may contribute or lead to a number of conditions and diseases.

- Dried or fresh fruit and vegetables, such as raisins, should be added about 15 minutes into the kneading cycle. If added at the beginning they will be shredded or mashed.

- Consider the moisture content of fresh fruit and vegetables and reduce the amount of water in the recipe accordingly. The flour's ability to absorb liquid is also influenced by the weather. Excess humidity in the air increases the moisture content of flour and may result in a denser, lower loaf.

Healthy Recipes

A breadmaker is simple to operate, requiring very little effort on your part. You know your breadmaker better than we do. If you don't, read the manual that came with it. Once you know your breadmaker, and the options it features, you simply need a good recipe.

The following pages provide wholesome recipes with healthful ingredients for wonderful bread baking. Simply follow our ingredient list with your own breadmaker instructions and enjoy the results.

Popcorn Bread

This wonderful bread usually evokes wonderful memories of afternoons at the movies or the fairgrounds. The result of this recipe is a truly unique taste, one that will probably become a family favorite.

1 ¼ cups (310 ml) **warm water**

2 tbsp **unpasteurized honey**

2 tbsp **sunflower or hazelnut oil**

2 ⅔ cups (660 ml) **whole wheat flour**

¾ cup (185 ml) **popcorn flour**

2 tbsp **gluten flour**

1 tsp **sea salt**

1 ½ tbsp **powdered milk**

4 tsp **active dry yeast**

To make the popcorn flour, put popped popcorn (about 4 cups) in a blender or food processor and grind until fine. If your breadmaker has a *whole wheat dough* cycle, use it for this recipe.

Makes a 1 ½-pound loaf

When you see this friendly teddy bear beside a recipe, you will know it is a recipe that children love!

Sour Cream and Onion Bread

This traditional combination of sour cream and onion makes up a tasty bread that's great for a regular sandwich or paté and cheese at a party.

½ **cup** (125 ml) **warm water**

1 cup (250 ml) **sour cream or kefir**

2 tbsp natural sugar crystals

3 cups (750 ml) **whole wheat flour**

1 tsp sea salt

2 tbsp wheat germ

⅓ **cup** (80 ml) **dried onion flakes**

2 tbsp gluten flour

2 tsp active dry yeast

Choose the *whole wheat dough* cycle on your breadmaker if it gives you the option.

Makes a 1 ½-pound loaf

onion

Natural Sugar

Natural sugar crystals may be equally substituted for the white sugar called in your recipes. There are many types of natural sugar crystals on the market. Some are superior to others simply because of the way they're made. We use either Sucanat or Rapadura, which is dried cane juice and totally unrefined. These natural sweeteners have a higher nutritional value than white sugar, with a natural rich flavor. Unlike the process used to make white refined sugar, the process used to make these natural sugars preserves the natural taste and nutrition, without preservatives or additives, and actually has a lower level of sucrose than refined sugar.

Hazelnut Sesame Bread

If you want to serve something a bit different, the Hazelnut Sesame Bread is both elegant and nutritious.

1 ⅛ **cups (280 ml) warm water**

1 **tbsp unpasteurized honey**

1 ¼ **cups (310 ml) whole wheat flour**

1 **cup (250 ml) bread flour**

1 **tbsp gluten flour**

⅔ **tsp sea salt**

½ **tbsp active dry yeast**

1 **tbsp sesame seeds**

1 ½ **tbsp sunflower seeds**

2 **tbsp hazelnuts or filberts, chopped**

Do not add the nuts and seeds in the beginning of the baking process. Your breadmaker manual will explain when and how to incorporate additions in your specific machine.

Makes a 1-pound loaf

honey

Bread has been a staple food for thousands of years, as is shown in the words of the Lord's Prayer: Give us this day our daily bread.

Potato Oat Bread

Just as mashed potatoes are considered comfort food, so is this bread. On a side plate with some homemade soup, or simple on its own with organic butter, the Potato Oat Bread is fabulous.

¾ **cup** (185 ml) **warm water**

1 **tbsp unpasteurized honey**

½ **cup** (125 ml) **mashed potatoes**

1 **large free-range egg**

1 ½ **cups** (375 ml) **whole wheat flour**

1 **cup** (250 ml) **bread flour**

½ **cup** (125 ml) **quick cooking oats**

1 **tsp sea salt**

4 **tbsp butter or coconut butter**

1 **tbsp active dry yeast**

2 **tbsp sunflower seeds**

Makes a 1 ½-pound loaf

potato

Multigrain Soy Bread

With this hearty recipe, you can enjoy your nutritious grains and protein at the same time.

1 ¼ cups (310 ml) **warm water**

1 **tbsp honey**

1 **tbsp olive or pistachio oil**

1 **cup** (250 ml) **whole wheat flour**

1 **cup** (250 ml) **bread flour**

⅓ **cup** (80 ml) **soy flour**

1 **tbsp nutritional yeast**

¾ **cup** (185 ml) **multigrain cereal**

2 **tbsp gluten flour**

2 **tsp sea salt**

2 **tsp active dry yeast**

If your breadmaker offers it, select the *three-dough* cycle.

Makes a 1 ½-pound loaf

If you're tired of cereal for breakfast this bread is a perfect substitute. With some jam on top (page 56) children are happy and healthy.

Sunflower Wheat Bread

No wonder the birds love their sunflower seeds. They taste delicious and provide more protein than most meat.

1 ⅛ **cups** (280 ml) **warm water**

3 **tbsp olive oil**

2 **tbsp honey**

1 ½ **cups** (375 ml) **whole wheat flour**

1 ½ **cups** (375 ml) **bread flour**

1 ½ **tsp sea salt**

½ **cup** (125 ml) **sunflower seeds**

3 **tsp gluten flour**

2 **tsp active dry yeast**

Select the *whole wheat dough* cycle if your breadmaker offers it.

Makes a 1 ½-pound loaf

Among many nutrients, sunflower seeds are rich in B vitamins, phosphorus and potassium. When shopping for sunflower seeds look for fresh medium-gray seeds that are sealed or kept in a refrigerator. Seeds should not be dark or multi-colored.

Country Seed Bread

This bread will evoke visions of people harvesting grains. The seeds in this bread supply vitamins, minerals and essential fatty acids (the good fats). Aside from its nutritional value is the fact that it simply tastes great.

1 ⅛ cups (280 ml) **warm water**

3 tbsp **olive or hazelnut oil**

2 tbsp **honey**

2 cups (500 ml) **whole wheat flour**

1 cup (250 ml) **bread flour**

1 ½ tsp **sea salt**

4 tbsp **flax seeds**

2 tbsp **sesame seeds**

1 tbsp **poppy seeds**

3 tsp **gluten flour**

1 ¾ tsp **active dry yeast**

Makes a 1 ½-pound loaf

Note: Using bread flour in your recipe will make your bread fluffy. Ask for bread flour at your local grocery store.

honey

Sunflower, flax, poppy and sesame seeds make excellent additions to bread for both taste and nutrition. They make breads look great too!

Sprouted Wheat Bread

Sprouts are an important part of the whole foods diet. They are especially helpful when fresh vegetables are out of season. The sprouts create a different and delicious bread.

½ **cup (125 ml) whole grain wheat**

1 ⅛ **cups (280 ml) warm liquid** (see directions)

2 tbsp olive or almond oil

1 tbsp dried cane sugar

2 ½ cups (375 ml) whole wheat flour

1 tsp sea salt

1 tbsp gluten flour

2 tsp active dry yeast

Soak the whole grain wheat in water until it sprouts (1 or 2 days). Take the liquid that is left over from the sprouts and top it up with warm water until you have the 1 ⅛ cups of liquid called for in the ingredient list.

Makes a 1 ½-pound loaf

34

Whole Wheat Kefir Bread

A fabulous bread for both taste and nutrition, this recipe is simple, simple, simple. If you've never tried kefir, you'll be glad you did. Everyone likes it, even children.

1 cup (250 ml) water

¾ **cup (185 ml) kefir**

1 tbsp butter or coconut butter

1 tbsp dried cane sugar

3 ¾ cups (935 ml) whole wheat flour

1 ½ tsp sea salt

1 ½ tsp active dry yeast

Makes 1 ½-pound loaf

Kefir

Kefir is a popular fermented milk product in many parts of the world, and is now gaining status in the West as a delicious alternative to yogurt. Many of the liver cleansing recipes call for kefir. If you have not yet discovered how easy it is to make kefir, you may substitute with sour cream or crème fraîche.

Cheese Bread

Everybody loves a good cheese bread, especially when it's served warm.

¾ **cups** (185 ml) **+2 tbsp water**

2 ½ **tbsp butter or coconut butter**

1 **tbsp unpasteurized honey**

½ **tsp sea salt**

1 **tsp dry mustard**

2 ½ **tbsp Parmesan cheese, grated**

1 ½ **tsp paprika**

1 ¼ **cups** (310 ml) **grated Gouda or Gruyère cheese, lightly packed**

2 ½ **tbsp minced onions or dried onion flakes**

1 **cup** (250 ml) **whole wheat flour**

1 ½ **cups** (375 ml) **bread flour**

2 **tsp active dry yeast**

Makes a 1-pound loaf

butter

Whole Wheat Bran Bread

The bran in this bread provides an extra kick of fiber, which is a necessary element in keeping the body clean and functioning optimally.

1 ⅛ **cups** (280 ml) **warm water**	¼ **cup** (60 ml) **bran**
2 **tbsp sunflower or almond oil**	1 ½ **cups** (375 ml) **whole wheat flour**
2 **tbsp unpasteurized honey**	1 **cup** (250 ml) **bread flour**
¾ **tsp sea salt**	2 ½ **tsp gluten flour**
	2 **tsp active dry yeast**

Makes a 1 ½-pound loaf

Rye Sourdough Starter

1 **tbsp active dry yeast**

2½ **cup** (625 ml) **warm water** (38°C)

2 **cups** (500 ml) **rye flour**

1 **tbsp unpasteurized honey**

For each cup of starter used, replenish the remaining starter by stirring in 1 cup of water, ¾ cup of rye flour and 1 tsp of honey. Cover with cheesecloth and let stand at room temperature for 1 day, or until bubbly, and then refrigerate. If not used within 10 days, stir in 1 tsp of honey. Repeat every 10 days unless starter is replenished in the meantime.

In a bowl, dissolve the yeast in ½ cup warm water. Add remaining warm water and stir in the rye flour and honey. Whisk ingredients together until just smooth. Cover with a cotton cheesecloth and let stand at room temperature for 5 to 10 days, stirring 2 to 3 times each day. Mixture should stand until it has a sour, fermented aroma (the warmer the room the faster the process). When the starter has fermented, transfer to a jar and cover with cheesecloth (do not use a metal lid) and refrigerate.

To use starter: Remove the starter from refrigerator and mix well. The cold starter should have the consistency of thin pancake batter. If it's too thick, thin it by adding water before measuring the amount needed for the recipe. Measure the amount needed and let it sit until it warms to room temperature.

Yields 2 ½ cups (625 ml)

Carrot Rye Bread

Who needs carrot cake, when you can bake a lovely carrot bread. This wonderful combination of healthful ingredients will fill your home with a memorable aroma that promises good food.

1 cup (250 ml) **water**

¾ **cup** (185 ml) **grated carrots**

2 tsp **dried cane sugar**

1 tbsp **butter or coconut butter**

1 tsp **sea salt**

2 ¼ **cups** (310 ml) **whole wheat flour**

¾ **cup** (185 ml) **rye flour**

3 tsp **gluten flour**

2 tsp **active dry yeast**

If your breadmaker gives you the option, select the *whole wheat* cycle to bake this bread.

Makes a 1 ½-pound loaf

carrot

Mozzarella Sundried Tomato Bread

Delivering a taste of Italy, this bread is always popular at a party or with wine for a romantic dinner for two.

⅞ cup (215 ml) **warm water**

½ cup (125 ml) **sundried tomatoes, chopped**

1 tbsp **unpasteurized honey**

2 tbsp **extra virgin olive oil**

1 cup (250 ml) **bread flour**

1 ¾ cup (435 ml) **whole wheat flour**

1 tsp **sea salt**

½ cup (125 ml) **Mozzarella cheese, grated**

1 tsp **garlic powder**

2 ½ tsp **active dry yeast**

Soak the sun dried tomatoes in warm water for 10 to 15 minutes. Drain and save the water to use as part of the ⅞ cup the ingredient list calls for. Use the *whole wheat* setting on your breadmaker, if you have that option.

Makes a 1 ½-pound loaf

tomato

Zucchini Bread

High in vitamins and low in calories, the zucchini in this recipe really makes the bread a tasty treat.

¾ **cup** (185 ml) **water**

¾ **cup** (185 ml) **grated zucchini**

3 **tbsp extra virgin olive oil**

I **tbsp honey**

I **tsp sea salt**

¼ **cup** (60 ml) **wheatgerm**

I ½ **cup** (375 ml) **whole wheat flour**

I ½ **cups** (375 ml) **bread flour**

I **tbsp gluten flour**

2 ½ **tsp active dry yeast**

Makes a 1 ½-pound loaf

Zucchini is high in vitamin A, which is important for eye health and skin. This summer squash is a healthy food overall and creates a wonderful bread.

Cashew Bread

High in potassium, magnesium and vitamin A, cashews offer a rich and tasty treat when included in this bread.

I ¼ cups (310 ml) **water**

I tbsp **unpasteurized honey**

I tbsp **butter or coconut butter**

2 cups (500 ml) **whole wheat flour**

I cup (250 ml) **bread flour**

I tbsp **gluten flour**

I ½ tsp **sea salt**

I ½ tsp **active dry yeast**

¾ cup (185 ml) **cashews, finely chopped**

Select the *sweetbread* cycle on your breadmaker, if it is an option. Don't forget to consult your breadmaker manual to see when it's best to add the cashews.

Makes a 1 ½-pound loaf

honey

Look for crisp and white cashews, and buy them whole as they stay fresh longer than cashew pieces.

Raisin Bread

Nothing beats toasted and buttered raisin bread.

1 cup (250 ml) + 1 tbsp milk

2 tbsp butter or coconut butter

1 tbsp natural sugar crystals or honey

1 ½ cups (375 ml) whole wheat flour

1 cup (250 ml) bread flour

1 ½ tsp sea salt

Zest of one lemon

1 ½ tsp active dry yeast

¾ cup (185 ml) raisins

If you have a *sweetbread dough* cycle on your breadmaker, select it for this recipe. Check you breakmaker manual to see when it's best to add the raisins.

Makes a 1 ½-pound loaf

organic milk

lemon

Greek Feta and Olive Bread

The popular combination of feta cheese and olives gives your taste buds a touch of Greece with this filling and fancy-looking bread.

1 cup (250 ml) **+2 tbsp milk**

½ **cup** (125 ml) **Feta cheese, crumbled**

⅓ **cup** (80 ml) **pitted kalamata olives, chopped**

2 tbsp water

1 tbsp butter or coconut butter

1 ½ cups (375 ml) **whole wheat flour**

½ **cup** (125 ml) **bread flour**

1 cup (250 ml) **rye flour**

1 tsp rosemary, dried or fresh

½ **tsp sea salt**

1 tsp active dry yeast

Select the *whole wheat* cycle if it's an option on your breadmaker.

Makes a 1 ½-pound loaf

organic milk

The Greeks and Italians have been consuming olive oil for centuries and are known for their low incidence of heart disease.

Tzatziki Rye Bread

Looking for something different you say? This bread fits the bill. The unbeatable garlic taste will have you making it regularly.

Bread

1 **cup** (250 ml) **sour dough starter** (page 38)

1 **cup** (250 ml) **Tzatziki**

½ **cup** (125 ml) **water** (including cucumber juice)

1 **tbsp honey**

1 ½ **cups** (375 ml) **rye flour**

1 ¼ **cups** (310 ml) **bread flour**

½ **cup** (125 ml) **whole wheat flour**

1 **tsp sea salt**

1 **clove garlic, crushed or finely grated**

1 **tsp dried dill**

1 **tbsp gluten flour**

1 **tsp active dry yeast**

Select the *whole wheat dough* cycle for this recipe, if available.

Makes a 1 ½-pound loaf

Tzatziki

1 **cup** (250 ml) **yogurt or kefir**

½ **cup** (125 ml) **natural sour cream**

½ **cucumber, shredded**

2 **cloves garlic, minced or finely grated**

1 **tbsp lemon juice**

1 **tsp dill**

Sea salt and freshly ground pepper, to taste

Cover a sieve with a cheesecloth and place over a bowl. Place yogurt or kefir and sour cream in sieve and drain for about 2 hours or in refrigerator overnight. Sprinkle salt over grated cucumber, let sit for 10 minutes, squeeze off juice and save for bread.

Combine cucumber with yogurt and sour cream mixture and add garlic, lemon juice, dill and pepper. Let sit for at least 1 hour.

Cranberry Jam

4 cups (1 L) cranberries

2 cinnamon sticks

2 star anise or ½ tsp ground anise

4 cloves or ¼ tsp ground cloves

1 orange, cut in segments

1 ½ cups (375 ml) dried cane sugar

½ cup (125 ml) red wine or orange juice

Zest of one lemon

Place all ingredients in medium-size pot and bring to a rapid boil. Let boil for a few minutes then reduce heat to medium and simmer for 25 minutes, or until jam begins to thicken. Remove from heat and let cool. If you have used whole star anise and/or whole cloves, remove now, along with the cinnamon sticks and remainder of orange pieces. Pour into hot, sterile jars and refrigerate.

cranberry

Strawberry-Kiwi Jam

4 cups (1 L) fresh or frozen strawberries, mashed to a pulp

6 kiwis, mashed to a pulp

½ cup (125 ml) unpasteurized honey

2 tbsp arrowroot powder (natural gelatin)

Dissolve arrowroot powder in ½ cup of the strawberry pulp. Bring remaining strawberry pulp to a boil. Remove from stove and add arrowroot/strawberry mixture. Bring to a boil and cook for 5 minutes, or until mixture starts to thicken. Remove from stove and let cool slightly.

Add honey and kiwi pulp. Taste for sweetness and add more honey if necessary (the honey does not serve as a preservative, it is only needed as a sweetener). Pour into hot, sterile jars and refrigerate.

kiwi

strawberry

Strawberry-kiwi jam is excellent with crêpes or as a sweetener for a kefir or yogurt/banana shake.

Spinach Spread

1 lb (500 g) spinach leaves

2 cloves garlic, minced

1 onion, chopped

2 tbsp cold-pressed olive oil

1 ½ cups (380 ml) kefir (or sourcream)

Pinch nutmeg

2 tbsp flax oil

Sea salt and freshly ground pepper, to taste

Blanch the spinach in boiling water for 2 minutes. Sauté garlic, onion and well-drained spinach in the olive oil for 3 minutes. Put sautéed mixture and the rest of the ingredients into a blender and mix on pulse setting for a chunky spread.

spinach

58

Sundried Tomato Spread

½ lb (250 g) sundried tomatoes

¼ cup (60 ml) pine nuts

¼ cup (60 ml) Asiago cheese, grated

1 tbsp fresh basil, chopped (or 1 tbsp pesto sauce)

Blend all ingredients in a blender until you have a smooth paste-like spread.

If you do not have sundried tomatoes, simply blanch ½ pound (250 g) of tomatoes, with 2 bay leaves and 2 cloves of garlic, for 3 minutes in boiling water. Rinse in cold water and drizzle with olive oil. Then add the rest of the recipe ingredients and blend.

Herb Butter

1 lb (500 g) **butter** (at room temperature)
1 tbsp parsley, chopped
1 tbsp thyme, chopped
1 tbsp rosemary, chopped
1 tbsp sage, chopped (or marjoram)
1 tbsp oregano, chopped
1 tbsp Braggs liquid
1 tbsp lemon juice

Blend all ingredients until smooth.

butter

parsley

Quark Spread

2 cups (500 ml) **quark** (or sour cream)
1 tbsp Braggs liquid
5 tbsp flax seed oil
Pinch nutmeg
1 tsp Herbamare vegetable salt
½ tsp fresh mint, chopped (or chives)
2 cloves garlic, minced

Blend all ingredients until smooth.

garlic

When breadmakers first appeared on the market people were truly excited about the possibility of making their own bread. Unfortunately, many of the machines were finicky and did not make bread baking as easy as it first appeared it would be. Since then, breadmakers have improved tremendously and allow us to bake trouble free bread with great success and little mess. Baking with the breadmaker is worth another try, for all the reasons we've stated in this book and more. We tried two different, well known, breadmakers. Both of them worked wonderfully. The only difference was the shape of the breads they produced.

We would like to thank Panasonic and West Bend who donated breadmakers for the making of this book.

All recipes have been tested in the *alive* kitchen, where the results were tasted and approved by the *alive* staff.

sources

for breadmakers:
Panasonic Canada Inc.
5770 Ambler Drive
Mississauga, ON
L4W 2T3
Tel: (905) 624-5505
Fax:(905) 238-2360
Email: panasonic@panasonic.ca

West Bend
400 Washington Street
West Bend, Wisconsin
53095 USA
Tel: (262) 334-6822
Web site: www.westbend.com

for kefir maker and flour mill:
Teldon of Canada Ltd.
7432 Fraser Park Drive
Burnaby, BC V5J 5B9
Tel: (604) 436-0545
Orders:1-800-663-2212
Fax: (604) 435-4862
E-mail: teldon@ultranet.ca

Bio Supply Ltd.
6-310 Goldstream Ave.
Victoria, B.C.
V9B 2W3
Toll Free: 1-888-225-3322
Tel: 250-478-3244
Fax: 250-478-3057
Email: biosupply@biosupply.com
Web site: www.biosupply.com

First published in 2000 by
alive books
7436 Fraser Park Drive
Burnaby BC V5J 5B9
(604) 435-1919
1-800-661-0303

Book Design:
    Liza Novecoski
Artwork:
    Terence Yeung
    Raymond Cheung
Food Styling:
    Fred Edrissi
Photography:
    Edmond Fong (recipe photos)
    Siegfried Gursche
Photo Editing:
    Sabine Edrissi-Bredenbrock
Editing:
    Sandra Tonn

Canadian Cataloguing in Publication Data

Alles, Silke and Janzen, Sieglinde
    Healthy Breads with the Breadmaker

(alive natural health guides, 13
ISSN 1490-6503)
ISBN 1-55312-014-0

Printed in Canada

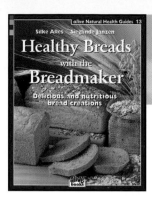

books

Natural
Your best source of

We hope you enjoyed **Healthy Breads with the Breadmaker**. There are 31 other titles to choose from in *alive*'s library of Natural Health Guides, and more coming soon. The first series of its kind in North America - now sold on 5 continents!

Self-Help Information

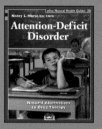
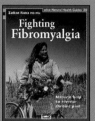

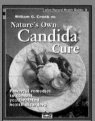
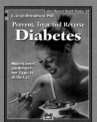

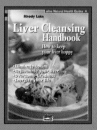

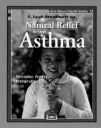

Healing Foods & Herbs

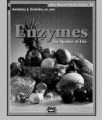

expert authors   •   easy-to-read information   •   tasty recipes